Skills On Studying

HELP IS ON THE WAY FOR:

Schoolwork

Written by Marilyn Berry
Pictures by Bartholomew

CHILDRENS PRESS ™

CHICAGO

Childrens Press
School and Library Edition

Producers: Ron Berry and Joy Wilt Berry
Editor: Orly Kelly
Consultant: Georgiana Burt
Design and Production: Abigail Johnston
Typesetting: Curt Chelin

So your teacher is really piling on the **schoolwork**!

Hang on! Help is on the way!

If you have a hard time

- doing schoolwork in class,
- doing schoolwork at home, or
- getting your schoolwork done on time,

. . . you are not alone!

Just in case you're wondering...

...why don't we start at the beginning?

WHY DO SCHOOLWORK?

There are many good reasons for schoolwork.

Practice makes perfect. People use this phrase often when talking about music or sports.

But the phrase "practice makes perfect" applies to schoolwork just as well.

Schoolwork shows what you know. It lets you and your teacher find out if you understand material being studied and new material being introduced.

It is always best to make sure you understand your current schoolwork *before* you move on to something new.

Schoolwork keeps you on your toes. Your teacher can be full of surprises, such as sudden questions and "pop" quizzes.

Staying on top of your schoolwork will keep you prepared for almost any surprise.

Doing your schoolwork lets you feel like one of the gang. You will get more out of school when you take an active part in classroom work.

When you do your schoolwork, you are better prepared to contribute in class.

Doing your schoolwork saves you from last-minute cramming. Studying for a test is much easier when you have kept up with your schoolwork.

Learning something a little at a time is much better than trying to learn it all at once.

Keeping up your schoolwork spruces up your report card. When you *don't* do your schoolwork, your grades will tend to slip.

When you *do* do your schoolwork, your grades will almost always improve.

CLASSWORK

Schoolwork in the classroom

When your teacher gives you an assignment to do in class, there are four things you should remember.

1. **Ask your teacher questions** to make sure you understand the assignment *before* you begin.

   Understanding the assignment can save you from a lot of extra work.

2. **If possible, do a small portion** of the assignment and have your teacher check it *before* you go on with the rest.

   Understanding the assignment can save you from having to do your work over again.

3. Get right to work.
It is a good idea to do the assignment while it is fresh in your mind. Also, getting right to work...

...keeps you out of trouble,

...allows you time for other activities,

...allows you time to work carefully and to avoid making careless mistakes,

...lets you avoid taking extra work home.

4. Make it fun. Classwork can be fun when...

- you make up games to play with yourself,
- you reward yourself for your hard work.

Here is a game you might try:

Beat the Clock

How to play:

- Look over the assignment.

- Guess how long it will take to complete.

- Do the assignment carefully, and after you have finished, check to see how long it took you.

The object of this game is to see how close you can come to your estimated time.

Here is another game you can play:

Perfection

How to play:

- Do the assignment carefully.

- Check your work for possible mistakes. Each mistake you find counts one point (the fewer the points, the better).

- Keep track of your score on each assignment. Try to get a lower score next time.

The object of this game is to complete an assignment without making any mistakes.

When you complete an assignment, reward yourself.

Take a short break. Stretch or simply relax for a few minutes. Get yourself a drink of water or take a little time to do something special.

Give yourself a treat. Set aside a part of your allowance to buy yourself a treat after school. Keep some treats on hand and reward yourself during recess or lunchtime.

HOMEWORK

Schoolwork at home

Homework will seem much easier if you are organized.

There are two steps to take to get organized:

STEP 1

Use an assignment book. Buy an inexpensive notebook, or make your own. To make your own assignment book you will need:

- a stack of plain paper
  5 ½ '' x 8 ½ ''
- poster board
- a paper punch
- yarn or brads
- crayons or felt pens

Instructions:

- Punch two holes on one side of the stack of paper, a few sheets at a time.

- Cut two pieces of poster board that measure slightly larger than the stack of paper and punch two holes on one side of them. (Make sure the holes all line up.)

- Put one piece of poster board under the stack of paper and one on top to make a cover for your book.

- Thread a piece of yarn through each hole of the book, and tie securely. Or, use two brads to hold the book together.

- Decorate the cover of your assignment book. Be sure to include your name and address in case the book is lost.

- To complete your assignment book you will need to fill in each page with the following information:

Subject _____ Due Date _____
Books needed _____
Materials needed _____

Explanation _____

Sample _____

Subject _____ Date Due _____
Books needed _____
Materials needed _____

Explanation _____

Sample _____

You should be able to fit two assignment forms on each side of the page.

Keep your assignment book handy at school and at home.

It will save you from a lot of wasted time and energy.

Write each assignment in your assignment book *when it is given*.

It is very difficult to remember the details of your assignments later on.

Ask your teacher questions to make sure you understand the assignment. Take notes in the explanation section of your assignment book.

Asking questions may save you from a lot of extra work.

If possible do a sample problem in the sample
section of your assignment book and have your
teacher check it.

This will help you to make sure that you do the
assignment correctly.

Before you leave school, check your assignment book to see what books and materials you will need to complete all your assignments.

Gather together any of these items you may not have at home.

Using an assignment book will make it easier to keep up with your homework and will help your life run more smoothly.

Planning your time after school. Planning your afternoons is easy if you use a simple time chart. All you need to make one is a pencil and a piece of paper.

Instructions:

- List the hours and half hours from the time you are out of school to the time you go to bed.

- Fill in any activities that you have already planned, such as dinner, chores, or bedtime.

Now, look through your assignment book, and, on a separate piece of paper, list all of your assignments in order of importance.

- Assignments that are due the next day should be at the top of your list.
- Difficult assignments should also be listed near the top. It is best to get them out of the way.

Estimate how much time each assignment will take. Finish filling in your time chart with your assignments. Any time left over is free time for you.

Now that you are organized, it's time to do your homework. Here are five things to keep in mind.

1. **The sooner you do your homework the better.** It is best to do your work while it is fresh in your mind.

   Also, you can enjoy other activities more when you get your work done first.

2. Make it fun. You can take the work out of homework if you:

• Make up games to play with yourself and others.

• Give yourself rewards. Have some kind of treat handy and set up your own reward system.

3. Give yourself a break. Especially when you have a lot of homework, it is important to take a break now and then.

Remember to keep your breaks occasional and short.

4. Check your work, or have someone check it for you.

Checking your work allows you to correct careless mistakes that might have been overlooked.

5. Put your homework in a safe place. After you have finished your homework, put it in a place where you won't forget it...

...or lose it.

KEEPING YOUR ASSIGNMENTS

When a teacher hands back a paper, you may be tempted to throw that paper away. *Don't*. Keep your papers. They may come in handy when you are studying for tests. They can also save you from doing a lot of extra work.

To get the most out of past assignments, there are two things you should do.

1. **Correct your work.** When your teacher hands back a paper, be sure to look it over and correct your mistakes. If your teacher has corrected your errors, make sure you understand where you went wrong.

Keeping past assignments is worthwhile only if they give you correct information.

2. **File your work.** After you have corrected any mistakes, put your assignments into a special file.

Keeping past assignments is worthwhile only if you can find them later when you need them.

Setting up your own filing system is easy and fun.

You will need:
- file folders—one for each subject,
- a shoe box to hold current file folders, and
- a larger box for storage of old file folders.

File folders are inexpensive, but if you have some extra poster board you can make your own.

Instructions:

- Cut a piece of poster board 12'' wide and 18'' long.
- Fold the board in half to 12'' by 9''. This will be the perfect size to hold your papers.
- Write the name of one of your subjects on the front of the folder.

Now, make one file folder for each one of your subjects at school.

The ideal box for holding your current file folders is a shoe box approximately 12½'' long (the deeper the better). Decorate your file box to make it personal and place it on your desk so that your papers will always be handy.

After your teacher has handed back an assignment and you have corrected it, put the paper in its proper file folder. Keep your current file folders in the file box on your desk.

To complete your filing system, you will need a larger box for storing old folders of papers from past classes. In order so save space, you may choose to keep only the more important papers.

It is fun to go through this box from time to time to look at the work you've done in the past. You'll be surprised at what you have learned.

OTHER THOUGHTS ABOUT SCHOOLWORK

With a little extra effort on your part, your schoolwork can go from good to great. Here are some simple tips to remember:

- **Keep it neat.** A neat paper is much easier to read and often gets a better grade than a messy paper.

- **Use proper form.** It usually takes the same amount of work and time to do an assignment the right way as it does to do it the wrong way. However, the benefits are much greater when you do it the right way.

- **Find a proper place to work.** You will do a better job and get more done if you do your homework in a place with no distractions.

Be sure to choose a place that has enough work space.

- **Hand your assignments in on time.** Don't waste your time thinking up creative excuses for late papers. Late papers usually get lower grades.

It is much better to do your work and hand it in on time!

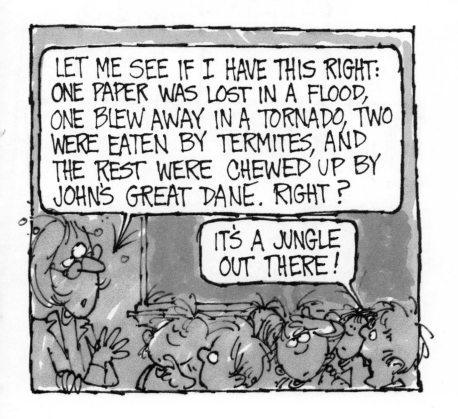

WARNING!

If you do the things in this book...

...you will probably become a better student!

THE END

About the Author
Marilyn Berry has a master's degree in education with a specialization in reading. She is on the staff as a producer and creator of supplementary materials at the Institute of Living Skills. Marilyn is a published author of books and composer of music for children. She is the mother of two sons, John and Brent.